SPIES!

Deep-Cover Spies AND Double-Crossers OF THE COLD WAR

REBECCA LANGSTON-GEORGE

Raintree is an imprint of Capstone Global Library Limited, a company incorporated in England and Wales having its registered office at 264 Banbury Road, Oxford, OX2 7DY – Registered company number: 6695582

www.raintree.co.uk
myorders@raintree.co.uk

Edited by Megan Atwood
Designed by Russell Griesmer
Picture research by Tracey Engel
Production by Steve Walker
Printed and bound in China

ISBN 978 1 4747 3620 6
20 19 18 17 16
10 9 8 7 6 5 4 3 2 1

British Library Cataloguing in Publication
A full catalogue record for this book is availa

Acknowledgements
We would like to thank the following for permission to reproduce photographs: Alamy: Chronicle, 40; SPUTNIK, 44; AP Photo: Charles Dharapak, 48; Getty Images: Archive Photos, 6, Bettmann, 14, 36, BRENDAN SMIALOWSKI/AFP, 27, Central Press, 8, Keystone-France/Gamma-Keystone, 50, New York Daily News Archive, 29, Time Life Pictures/The LIFE Picture Collection, 11; Newscom: akg-images, 18 (both), Crown/Mirrorpix, 30, Everett Collection, 21, 46, HUGH VAN ES UPI Photo Service, 56, Keystone Pictures USA/Zuma Press, 38, UPPA/Photoshot, 24; Shutterstock: Alexey Fyodorov, cover and 1 (Red Square silhouette), Benoit Daoust, cover (male silhouette), Black Russian Studio, cover and 1 (Capitol Building), Ensuper, design element, Fedorov Oleksiy, design element, Freedom_Studio, design element, Here, design element, lenaer, cover (female face), phokin, design element, Rangizzz, cover and interior design element, Reddavebatcave, design element, SkillUp, design element, STILLFX, cover and 1 (flag), Venera Salman, cover and interior design element, Vladitto, design element, wawritto, cover and 1 (hammer and sickle)

We would like to thank Joseph Fitsanakis, PhD of Coastal Carolina University for his invaluable help in the preparation of this book.

CONTENTS

The Cold War was a period of time when two superpowers with two different ideologies when head to head: the United States, whose ideology was democracy, and the Soviet Union, whose ideology was communism.

In World War II, the Soviet Union and the United States fought together to defeat Germany and Adolf Hitler. However, the United States was uneasy with the dictatorship of Joseph Stalin in the Soviet Union and the principles of communism in general. The Soviet Union was upset and nervous about the United States' advanced technology and atomic weapons, which they'd used against Japan at the end of World War II. Soon after the end of the war the tensions between the two countries overflowed.

In 1947 US president Harry S Truman announced the Truman Doctrine. He pledged the support – economic, military and political – of the United States to any nation threatened by authoritarian regimes or forces. This sparked the years of the Cold War where the two superpowers were locked in a struggle over whose ideology would win.

The fight played out in a number of conflicts primarily fought by other nations. Among the many conflicts sparked by this struggle were the civil war in Korea (1950–1953), the long, drawn-out conflict between North and South Vietnam (1955–1975) and the Cuban Missile Crisis (in October of 1962).

Additionally, the United States and the Soviet Union were locked in two other conflicts: the space race and the arms race. The space race was a competition to see which superpower could gain ground in the exploration of space and build the most technologically advanced equipment. When the Soviet Union launched the first satellite, Sputnik, in 1957, the race was on. In 1969, the United States landed on the moon, effectively winning the space race.

One of the most intense aspects of the war, however, was the "arms race." Throughout the Cold War, the Soviet Union and the United States kept escalating the number and scope of the weapons they were stockpiling, including nuclear weapons. The world teetered on the edge of nuclear war. The concept of Mutually Assured Destruction (MAD) – or, the idea that if one country attacked the other with nuclear weapons, the other country would too, ending both countries – seemed to be the only thing keeping the world from total destruction.

Finally, in 1991, the Soviet leader, Mikhail Gorbachev, began dismantling the Soviet Union and its communist economic policies. Countries that had been conquered by the Soviet Union regained their independence and the Soviet Union was dismantled. There are now 15 separate countries that were once part of the Soviet Union.

Both superpowers of the Cold War relied heavily on intelligence gathered by spies. These deep-cover, often double-crossing, operatives played huge roles in the successes and failures of the Cold War. This book explores the lives and deeds of a few of the most influential spies of the Cold War.

Gary Powers flew spy planes over the Soviet Union.

CHAPTER 1

GARY POWERS: THE SPY WHO GOT SWAPPED

Francis Gary Powers should have been suspicious of the job offer right from the start. It began with a mysterious invitation from his commander to apply for another assignment, then a secret evening meeting at a hotel where he was told to ask for Mr. Collins. The offer came with a big salary, more than double what he earned as a pilot for the US Air Force, but Mr. Collins wouldn't tell him exactly what the job was. It was patriotic. It involved travel out of the country. It involved flying.

As Gary Powers soon found out, it also involved a lot of danger. His new employer was the Central Intelligence Agency (CIA). His new job was to fly a just-created secret aircraft called the U-2. The aircraft was a light plane with a fast jet engine that allowed it to fly higher than any other plane and stay in the air for a very long time. The U-2 flew so high that it was nearly invisible and undetectable by radar systems. It was believed that an enemy's surface-to-air missiles (SAMs) couldn't reach it.

The U-2 was the plane Gary Powers used for spying.

Gary was given an alias: Francis G Palmer. Under this alias,

he registered at a Washington DC hotel in January 1956 and

waited by the phone for instructions from the mysterious Mr.

Collins. For the next three months Gary moved from hotel to

hotel and room to room for meetings and training sessions. Each

time before they spoke, Mr. Collins turned the radio on just in

case the room was bugged. During this time the CIA performed

lie detector tests as well as rigorous physical and psychological

tests on Gary. They had to make sure he could endure the

physical strain of flying the U-2 and the emotional stress of not

being able to talk about his job.

DID YOU KNOW?

The KGB was the security and
intelligence agency, and secret
police, of the Soviet Union from
1954 to 1991.

TRAINING FOR DUTY

After months of tests and meetings, Gary was sent to a secret training base in the Nevada desert where he learned to fly the U-2. Before he could take to the air, he had to be trained to breathe correctly in high altitudes and engage in hours of "pre-breathing" exercises with pure oxygen. The U-2 was unlike anything he had ever flown before.

The ultra-light plane contained emergency supplies, including a parachute, inflatable life raft, warm clothing, compass, knife and money from various countries. It also included an item for extreme emergencies: a hollow silver dollar coin containing a suicide pin coated in curare, a lethal poison. It could be used in the event the pilot crashed and was taken into custody in a hostile country.

Gary would be flying over very hostile territory indeed. The Soviet Union shot down pilots who wandered into their territory accidentally, and Gary's flights over the USSR would be no accident. The United States had designed the U-2 specifically to fly over the USSR undetected for a job they called Operation Overflight. The plane was equipped with a special camera to take pictures of military bases, missile launch sites, early warning system facilities and other places the Soviets preferred to keep secret.

Gary Powers spied on the Soviet
Union for years with the U-2.

After being transferred overseas, Gary made practice runs from US military bases in Turkey and Pakistan, photographing things along the Soviet border without crossing the boundary. After several months of practising over friendly territory, Gary was ready for the real mission: penetrating the Soviet border to spy. For the next four years he flew many U-2 flights over the USSR, taking surveillance pictures for both the CIA and the National Security Agency (NSA).

After years of flying the most secret aircraft in the world over hostile territory, the mission had begun to feel routine for Gary. It became a job like any other job. But all that changed in the spring of 1960 during a fateful flight. Gary didn't know it, but it was to be his last U-2 flight. The United States had long underestimated the Soviets' radar technology. But, it was about to become evident that the Soviets could detect the U-2, and that they had been perfecting their surface-to-air missile range. Gary was sent to Peshawar, Pakistan, where the flight would originate, but his flight order was delayed several times over the next few days. The flight was finally authorized and he left Pakistan at 6.26 a.m. on 1 May 1960. His flight would carry him over Russia and end in Norway.

Four hours into the flight, Gary heard a bang as the U-2 shook and an orange flash lit up the sky. Although the missile did not hit the plane directly, the sonic waves resulting from the nearby explosion proved catastrophic. The plane spiralled down. Gary tried to activate the ejection seat, but his legs were trapped. The canopy overhead sailed away. Mirrors snapped off. As bits of the plane broke loose, Gary freed his legs and climbed out. His orange-and-white parachute ballooned above him and he floated down into enemy territory.

FROM PILOT TO PRISONER

On the way down he had the presence of mind to rip up the maps he was carrying. He also placed the sheathed needle from the silver dollar in his pocket in case he needed it later. He saw a car coming towards him. Upon landing, he was surrounded by villagers. A man emerged from the car and seized his gun. From his bizarre arrival out of the sky and the letters "U.S.A." on the gun handle, they quickly identified Gary as an American pilot. The men placed Gary in the car and drove him to the police station near the Russian city of Sverdlovsk. There Gary watched as a flood of people arrived, each carrying a bit of his destroyed plane.

He was taken into custody and his suicide pin was confiscated. Then he was flown to Moscow for questioning. The questioning continued all day, every day, for 61 days. At night he was locked in a prison cell. He had received no training on what to do in the event of a capture other than instructions on using the suicide pin. The only other advice he remembered was, "You might as well tell them everything because they're going to get it out of you anyway." Gary decided to tell the truth when it came to things the Soviets could either easily guess or confirm with the broken U-2 in their possession.

HOLLOW ITEMS

Hollow items like the nickel Rudolf Abel, a Soviet spy, used to hide microfilm and microdots are nothing new. Spies throughout the centuries have hollowed out everyday items and used them to conceal their secrets. Small, dead birds were once cleaned and prepared to hide messages. Cigarette lighters, hair and shaving brush handles, wine corks and pipes all look innocent but can be used to hide secrets. Spies aren't the only people who hide their secrets in hollow items. The famous magician Harry Houdini performed daring magic tricks using a key hidden in his hollow shoe heel to escape from chains.

He was charged with the state crime of espionage, tried in a Soviet court and, on his 31st birthday, found guilty. Because he cooperated, Francis Gary Powers was given a lenient sentence: 10 years in a Russian prison.

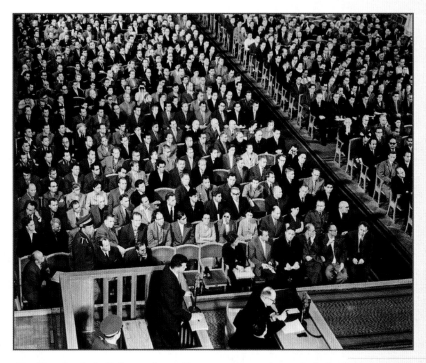

In the Soviet Union, Gary Powers was put on trial for spying.

Taken to Vladimir Prison east of Moscow to serve his term, he was housed with cellmate Zigurd Kruminsh, a Latvian who spoke both Russian and English. Gary's only communication with the outside world came from Soviet radio and newspapers. At first Zigurd translated for him. Later Zigurd taught him enough

Russian so he could understand some of the news himself. Gary was also allowed to receive post from his wife and parents.

Gary's father, Oliver Powers, not only wrote to his son in prison, he also wrote to another prisoner who he thought might be able to help his son: Colonel Rudolf Abel. Abel, whose real name was Vilyam Fisher, had been incarcerated in a US prison in 1957 for being a Soviet spy. He had transmitted information to the Soviets in various ways, such as by hiding microfilm photos in hollow nickels. Powers wrote to Abel to encourage him to talk Soviet officials into a prisoner exchange, swapping Abel for Gary. James Donovan, Colonel Abel's US defence lawyer, thought this was a very good idea.

THE EXCHANGE

On 7 February 1962, a year and nine months into his sentence, Gary Powers returned from a trip to the bathroom to find two KGB officers standing outside his prison cell. The KGB colonel asked Gary if he'd like to go to Moscow the following day. Like the mysterious Mr. Collins, the KGB man would reveal no more. But Gary knew something unusual was up when a guard brought in a small suitcase and told him to pack.

On arriving in Moscow, Gary thought he would be dropped off at the US Embassy. Instead he was informed they were flying to East Germany. On 10 February 1962, the KGB drove Gary

Powers to the Glienicke Bridge, which connected Potsdam, East Germany, to West Berlin in West Germany. At 8.20 a.m. Gary Powers followed five men onto the bridge with armed guards behind him. Across the bridge in the distance he saw another group of men approaching.

Both groups stopped just short of the middle. A man Gary recognized from the U-2 program walked up to him. "What was your high school football coach's name?" he asked. The United States wanted to make sure they weren't getting an imposter before turning Abel over to the KGB. But Gary couldn't, for the life of him, remember the answer he had provided years ago on the forms he had filled out. Had he come this far to be turned back for not remembering the answer to the code question? Thankfully he could provide the names of his wife, his mother and his dog, which convinced them he was the right person.

Gary waited as the KGB performed a similar interview with Rudolf Abel. When both sides were satisfied, the KGB colonel pushed Francis Gary Powers towards the west side of the bridge. He was free.

DID YOU KNOW?

Another US citizen, Frederic L Pryor,
was released at Checkpoint Charlie,
a guarded crossing between East and
West Berlin, at the same time as the
exchange of Gary Powers for Rudolf
Abel. Before the Berlin Wall was built,
Pryor conducted university research in
East Berlin. He was held on suspicion
of espionage by the East Germans,
though he was merely a student.

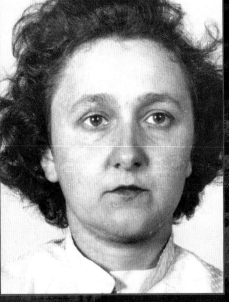

Julius and Ethel Rosenberg sparked much controversy in the United States and around the world.

CHAPTER 2

JULIUS AND ETHEL ROSENBERG: RED SCARE SPIES

For over 60 years, Julius and Ethel Rosenberg have been known as notorious Soviet spies who lived and worked in the United States. However, the complicated path that ended in their arrest shows a more complex story. What became of the Rosenbergs to this day remains controversial.

It all started with a KGB codebook found in Finland during World War II. The codebook eventually allowed the Federal Bureau of Investigation (FBI) to read communications intercepted from the Soviet Union. One document they deciphered was a report on the Manhattan Project by German-born British physicist Klaus Fuchs. Fuchs was one of the principal scientists who worked on the atomic bomb for the United States.

When the British Security Service confronted Fuchs in early 1950 with the codebook evidence of his treachery, he confessed. He admitted to spilling US and British atomic secrets to the Soviets. Under questioning, Fuchs said he passed his information along to a handler known as Raymond. After some investigation, the FBI discovered that Raymond was really Harry Gold, a US citizen who worked as a chemist. Gold had become a spy for the Soviet Union. The FBI arrested Gold and grilled him for the names of his other contacts. He confessed and mentioned an arranged meeting with a soldier stationed at Los Alamos who lived in Albuquerque, New Mexico. Gold couldn't remember the soldier's name but described his appearance, the neighborhood he lived in and his wife's name.

A FAMILY OF SPIES

From Gold's information, the FBI identified the soldier as David Greenglass. Greenglass had worked as an assistant foreman in the atomic bomb high explosives unit in Los Alamos. When questioned, Greenglass admitted passing secret atomic information to Harry Gold.

David Greenglass wasn't finished, though: he named his own family members, the Rosenbergs, as spies as well. Greenglass said that Julius Rosenberg – married to David's sister, Ethel – had set up the meeting with Gold. According to Greenglass (though his claims varied), he and his wife, Ruth, dined at the Rosenbergs' New York home one night during Greenglass' military leave. Greenglass claimed that during that dinner, Julius Rosenberg talked him into writing down everything he knew about Los Alamos and the atomic bomb.

David Greenglass was arrested for spying and soon pointed to
Julius and Ethel Rosenberg as fellow spies.

Also according to David Greenglass, Julius said he would

arrange for a courier – Harry Gold – to pick up Greenglass'

notes when he returned home to New Mexico. Since neither

David Greenglass nor his wife had ever met Harry Gold, Julius came up with a way for the Greenglasses to recognize the unknown courier. Julius tore the front label off a box of gelatin and cut it into two puzzle pieces. He gave one puzzle piece to the Greenglasses. Later, Harry Gold arrived in Albuquerque and showed the other half of the gelatin label to the Greenglasses. David Greenglass gave him the notes on Los Alamos and the atomic bomb. In return, Harry Gold gave David Greenglass £400.

David and his wife, Ruth, along with Ethel and Julius Rosenberg, had all been members of the Communist Party years earlier. Even during the Red Scare, the Rosenbergs held Communist Party meetings at their home and encouraged their friends and neighbors to attend. According to David Greenglass, Julius began spying for the Soviet Union.

Greenglass reported that while Julius was employed in the Signal Corps he stole fuses and other small weaponry parts as well as instruction manuals. He served as a courier, picking up drops at a cinema and delivering items to a Soviet agent. Greenglass claimed Julius rented a secret apartment from which he ran his spy ring and photographed secret documents. As Julius became more involved with the party, he and Ethel cancelled their subscriptions to communist newspapers and dropped their party memberships so as to not arouse any suspicion.

On 17 July 1950, as the Rosenbergs' older son sat listening to *The Lone Ranger* on the radio, the FBI arrested Julius Rosenberg in

DID YOU KNOW?

Many years later David Greenglass changed his story, saying that his wife, Ruth, had done the typing, so he had implicated Ethel to save Ruth. Afterwards he claimed he couldn't remember who had done what.

his apartment. He was charged with recruiting David Greenglass into espionage in 1944. Unlike the others arrested, Julius Rosenberg did not confess and refused to name his conspirators.

David Greenglass also implicated his sister, Ethel Rosenberg, in the spy ring, insisting she had typed some of the documents passed to Harry Gold.

Evidence against Ethel was weak, but in an effort to pressure Julius to talk, Ethel was arrested on 11 August 1950, following a grand jury investigation. She was not even allowed to make childcare arrangements for her and Julius' two sons, Michael and Robert.

The Rosenberg children comfort each other during their parents' trial.

THE TRIAL OF THE CENTURY

On 6 March 1951, the Rosenberg trial began. They were charged with conspiracy to commit espionage, a charge that could result in the death penalty. Both Julius and Ethel proclaimed their innocence. They refused to answer some of the questions posed to them, citing their Fifth Amendment right (the right to not be witnesses against themselves). During jury deliberations a lone juror at first held out against conviction because his conscience couldn't bear the idea of a mother of two young boys being executed. By the next morning that juror yielded and the Rosenbergs were found guilty.

RED SCARE

Following World War II, as the Soviet Union's power and influence grew, an anti-communist attitude and widespread fear of Soviet espionage spread across the United States. Fuelled by hearings of the House Un-American Activities Committee, many Americans faced accusations of being communists or affiliating with communists. In Hollywood entertainers suspected of being "reds" (so-called because the Soviet Union's flag was red) were blacklisted and couldn't find work. Many union leaders, college professors, government employees, those suspected of being gay and numerous other groups of people were hauled before the House Un-American Activities Committee and questioned about their loyalty to the United States. Senator Joseph McCarthy added fuel to the fire by claiming to have a list of spies who were members of the Communist Party, though in reality, there was no such list.

Before sentencing Julius and Ethel Rosenberg to death, Judge Irving Kaufman said:

"I believe your conduct in putting into the hands of the Russians the A-bomb years before our best scientists predicted Russia would perfect the bomb has already caused, in my opinion, the Communist aggression in Korea, with the resultant casualties exceeding fifty thousand and who knows but that millions more of innocent people may pay the price of your treason."

The Rosenbergs were the only defendants in the atomic spy trials to receive the death penalty, because they alone refused to name others. In exchange for testifying against the Rosenbergs, David Greenglass was sentenced to only 15 years in prison. In separate trials, Harry Gold was given 30 years, and Klaus Fuchs received 14 years. All of them later had their sentences greatly reduced.

For more than two years the Rosenbergs appealed their case. The appeal went all the way to the Supreme Court. On 14 June 1953, their 10-year-old son, Michael Rosenberg, delivered a handwritten letter to a guard at the White House. In it he begged President Eisenhower to grant his mummy and daddy clemency.

The court granted a temporary stay of execution on 17 June 1953. In response to the stay, more than 21,000 telegrams flooded into the White House asking for clemency. Thousands

> Dear Mr. President,
> Please don't leave my brother and I without a Mommy and Daddy.
> They have always been good to us. We love them very much.
> Michael and Robert Rosenberg
> 36 Laurel Hill Terrace
> New York, N.Y.

The Rosenbergs' son Michael wrote a letter to President Eisenhower.

of protesters picketed around the White House, demanding the execution be permanently overturned.

The following day was the Rosenbergs' 14th wedding anniversary. They spent the day writing letters and drafting their wills. The final decision on whether they would live or die was about to be handed down. In preparation, newspapers even had two different headlines standing by: "Rosenbergs Executed" and "Rosenbergs Saved." But there was to be no salvation for the Rosenbergs. On 19 June 1953, the Supreme Court reversed the stay, allowing the execution to go ahead.

The executions were set for 11.00 p.m. on Friday 19 June 1953. Hoping for an extension, the Rosenbergs' lawyer argued that a death sentence after sundown on a Friday desecrated the Jewish Sabbath. In response the warden moved the execution time forwards to 8.00 p.m. Julius and Ethel were allowed to spend their last afternoon of life together with a wire mesh wall separating them. They wrote a letter to their children. With their execution time moved forwards,

ROBERT AND MICHAEL MEEROPOL

After Julius and Ethel Rosenberg were executed, their sons, Robert and Michael, were adopted by Anne and Abel Meeropol. For decades, the Rosenberg brothers (now Meeropol brothers) fought to prove their parents, Julius and Ethel, were innocent. After a convicted Cold War spy released a statement in 2008, however, the brothers now believe their father was a Soviet spy. What he gave to the Soviets, though, did not amount to stealing atomic secrets, they say. The brothers also maintain that their mother, Ethel, was innocent and framed in order to get Julius to talk.

they did not eat a last meal. At 7.20 p.m. they were separated.

Before following her husband to the electric chair in New York's Sing Sing Prison, Ethel wrote a final letter to her lawyer, Manny Bloch, ending with the words, "We are the first victims of American Fascism."

Newspapers followed the Rosenbergs' case closely.

George Blake became one of the most notorious double agents of the Cold War.

CHAPTER 3

GEORGE BLAKE: JAILBIRD SPY

George Behar was born into a multicultural Dutch family: one that loved all things British. His Turkish father, Albert, married a Dutch woman and settled in the Netherlands. Albert became a naturalized British citizen and proudly named his son after the British king, George VI. He even changed his family's last name to Blake to make it sound more English. So, perhaps it was fortunate that Albert didn't live to see his scandalous son's name splashed across British newspaper headlines.

Following his father's death, George was sent to Cairo to live with relatives. His mother hoped he would have better educational opportunities in Egypt. There he learned French and English, in addition to his native Dutch.

Despite living in Egypt, he visited his family in the Netherlands whenever he could. It was during one such visit to his grandmother in May 1940 that the Germans invaded the Netherlands. His mother and sister, in another town, escaped to Britain, thinking he would soon follow.

Because he was a British citizen and the British were at

war with the Germans, George was taken into custody by the Germans and interned in a prisoner-of-war camp. But since he was only 16 years old, they soon released him. He wasn't old enough to be considered a threat. His prison experience, along with the invasion of the Netherlands, made George Blake angry enough to fight back. He joined the Dutch Resistance and carried secret packages and information across the country. With help from the Resistance, he plotted his escape to Britain to join his mother and sister. Along his escape route he travelled the Dutch countryside and stayed at safe houses. He was smuggled across the border to Spain, only to be imprisoned again, this time by Spanish authorities. Though Spain was officially neutral during the war, they collaborated with Nazi Germany and guarded their borders against those trying to escape German occupation.

ADVENTURE AND SECRETS

After holding George in captivity for months, Spanish authorities located his mother and he was finally released to travel to Britain. Upon arriving, George Blake volunteered to serve in the Royal Navy. After completing his training he applied to work in Special Services because he liked the idea of adventure and secrets. Once he passed the interviews and language tests, his knowledge of the Dutch Resistance landed George an assignment with the Dutch section of the British Secret Intelligence Service.

After World War II ended, the British Secret Intelligence Service sent George to language school to learn a fourth language: Russian. Following the completion of his course, George expected to be placed in an Eastern bloc country, controlled by the Soviet Union, to use his new language skills. Instead, he was surprised when he was placed in South Korea in 1948. It was an event that would alter the course of his life.

Shortly after George arrived, North Korea crossed the 38th parallel and invaded South Korea on 25 June 1950. Within days, George Blake was captured and put in a prisoner-of-war camp because he was a British citizen. While imprisoned for a year and a half, George became convinced the communist ideology was correct. He turned against his adopted homeland. One day he handed his Korean guard a note written in Russian and addressed to the Soviet Embassy, asking for a meeting.

At the meeting, George Blake offered to betray Britain and work as a double agent for the Soviets. The Soviets could hardly refuse his offer. After all, he was already a spy who spoke fluent Russian. He refused to accept any payment for his services, stating later, "I did what I did for ideological reasons, never for money." When he was released from prison with other POWs and returned to Britain, the first thing he did was meet with the British Secret Intelligence Service to resume his intelligence work. A few weeks later, he travelled to the Netherlands and met with his new KGB handler.

He was given a small Minox camera to photograph British documents. He worked overtime to comb through classified files for information his Soviet handler could use. Every three to four weeks he met his contact near a London Underground station to deliver information. During their clandestine meetings, George Blake revealed the names of other British spies to the KGB as well as any KGB double agents working for the British. In doing so, he doomed many of his fellow spies to death.

When George was reassigned to West Berlin, he was able to bring with him a stunning piece of intelligence for his Soviet friends in East Berlin. The British, along with the Americans, were building a tunnel to conceal phone-tapping equipment. The equipment would allow them to eavesdrop on communications at the Soviet Army headquarters. For years, the British thought their tunnel was a rousing success. Finally, the Soviets "discovered" the tap in 1956 and the operation was shut down. The KGB had known about the tap all along thanks to their double agent.

George Blake was one of the most successful double agents ever, but in 1960 George's own game caught up to him. The spy who had double-crossed dozens of his fellow spies was caught when a Polish spy defected to the United States and named George Blake as a double agent. George was called back to Britain and questioned for several days. He finally cracked when he was asked if he had defected under the duress of torture during his

DID YOU KNOW?

Following World War II, Germany was
divided into two sections. West Germany
was occupied by Britain, the United
States and France. It was run as a
capitalist state. East Germany was
occupied by the Soviet Union and run as
a socialist state. A wall in Berlin with
guarded checkpoints divided West Berlin
from East Germany from 1961 to 1989.

Korean imprisonment. He yelled, "No, nobody tortured me! No, nobody blackmailed me! I myself approached the Soviets and offered my services..."

SORRY? NOT SORRY

George was arrested. During the sentencing at his trial his lawyer wanted to say that George was "deeply sorry for all he had done," but George refused to allow it, saying it was untrue. He felt what he had done was right. The British court sentenced him to

WIRETAPPING

In George Blake's day, all phones were hardwired into buildings. To "tap" them, an electrical wire had to be installed to allow a person or people to listen in on conversations. If the wires were found, the victim knew his phone had been tapped. Today it's even easier to tap into both landline and mobile phones. No wires need to be installed. Digital signals just have to be diverted so a third party can listen in. This makes it almost impossible for victims to know their phones have been tapped.

Wiretapping is still a spy technique used today.

42 years in jail. The newspapers had a field day, claiming, in error, George Blake received one year for every British spy he betrayed.

Imprisoned for the fourth time in his life, George Blake decided he would not stay for long. He befriended fellow inmate Sean Bourke. When Sean was released, the two hatched George's escape plan. Sean created a rope ladder with knitting needle rungs, which he slung over the prison wall. While most of the guards and prisoners were attending a movie, George Blake climbed over the wall and into Sean's waiting car. Another friend hid him in a secret compartment of a van. They travelled all the way to the East Berlin checkpoint, and from there the Soviets transported Blake to the Soviet Union.

George Blake was welcomed into Soviet life with an elegantly furnished house, a personal housekeeper and chauffeur and a lifetime pension for his services. In his new comfortable life, he took a job in Soviet publishing and later wrote a book for a British publisher about his life as a double-crossing spy. It became a best-seller. But, the joke turned out to be on him. After only receiving one payment, the British courts stepped in and stopped him from receiving any further money from book sales, ruling he could not profit from his crimes. So, the double-crossing spy got double-crossed in the end.

Janet Chisholm became an important spy for the British government.

CHAPTER 4

JANET CHISHOLM: THE BABY BUGGY SPY

Janet Anne Deane Chisholm never intended to be a spy. But her life changed when she married one. She met her spy husband while she was working as a secretary in the British Intelligence Office. Her husband, Ruari Chisholm, became the British MI6 head of a station in Moscow. MI6 gathered intelligence from foreign countries. Officially his job title was embassy visa officer, but it was merely a cover for his intelligence work.

The posting to the Soviet Union was a welcome one to Janet, even though the British Secret Intelligence Service considered living in Moscow a hardship. She was no stranger to living in locations outside of Britain. Her father had been a British Royal Engineer and she was born at the foot of the Himalaya Mountains in the British Indies in 1929. She already knew Russian because she'd learned it at boarding school in England. All in all, Janet was well prepared for life in Moscow and the unexpected spy

Janet Chisholm felt at home in Russia.

adventure that awaited her there.

Quick-thinking and levelheaded, Janet was the perfect "cut-out," or go-between, for her husband when Russian Colonel Oleg Penkovsky decided to turn against the Soviet Union. Penkovsky felt that Soviet leader Nikita Khrushchev's aggressive stockpiling of weapons would lead to another world war. However, Penkovsky couldn't risk being seen with a known employee of the British Embassy like Ruari, so Janet took his place. She would be the contact who would do "live-drop" deliveries from Penkovsky.

Janet's first meeting with Oleg Penkovsky was arranged
by travelling businessman and British spy Grenville Wynne.
Wynne met Penkovsky and gave him a Minox camera and film to
photograph documents. He showed Penkovsky a picture of Janet
Chisholm, code-named Anne, and directed him to meet Janet at a
Moscow park on Tsvetnoy Boulevard on a prearranged date.

AN AFTERNOON AT THE PARK

On Sunday 2 July 1961, Janet brought her three small children
to the park for some summer sun. When they sat down on a
bench, Penkovsky approached and chatted with Janet and the
children like a grandfatherly man. He patted one of her blonde
children on the head and offered the child a box of Russian
chocolates. The box contained seven rolls of undeveloped Minox
film and photocopies of Soviet missile reports. Janet thanked him
for his kindness to the children and put Penkovsky's box in her
baby buggy. She covered the fake chocolates with a blanket and
pulled an identical box of real chocolates from the buggy, which
she offered to her children. This was the first of many exchanges
the two made.

While a couple of strolls in the park with candy wouldn't
arouse the KGB's suspicions, too many certainly would, so Janet
and Penkovsky had to vary their routine. After her ballet class,

Janet sometimes stopped in a secondhand store to browse through the used china and crystal. Penkovsky, code-named Hero, would enter, wait for her to notice him, then leave the store. Janet followed him at a distance until he entered an apartment building stairwell or alley for their brief meetings. If anyone walked by when they were together, Penkovsky and Janet embraced and acted like lovers as he slipped cigarette packets containing photo film and documents into Janet's shopping bag.

After one of their hand-off meetings, Penkovsky noticed a suspicious car making a U-turn on a one-way street. Two men in dark overcoats were following Janet in a car. Penkovsky became nervous, fearing Janet had been made, or identified, as a spy. He suggested they change their operation from clandestine meetings to social meetings at embassy cocktail parties. Cocktail parties were common events in which embassy employees and their families mingled with local dignitaries like Penkovsky, so he thought their casual social interactions wouldn't arouse suspicion.

PARTIES ARE TIRING

At one party, Janet, then seven months pregnant, was "introduced" to Colonel Penkovsky by the host. Penkovsky said, "You must be feeling tired. Why don't you rest for a few minutes in the hostess' bedroom?" Janet asked the hostess to lie down, blaming her tiredness on her pregnancy. A few minutes later Penkovsky asked the hostess to show him her lovely home. When they came to the bedroom and found Janet lying down, Penkovsky walked up to the bed, apologized for disturbing her, turned around and flashed a cigarette packet filled with information behind his back. Janet took it without the hostess being none the wiser.

Janet gave the missile reports and film concealed inside the cigarette packets and sweet boxes to her husband, Ruari. They never spoke of the operation out loud in their home in case the

LIVE-DROPS, BRUSH PASSES AND DEAD DROPS

A live-drop is when a spy hands documents or goods to his or her handler in an inconspicuous way, while acknowledging each other. Janet Chisholm and Oleg Penkovsky used empty chocolate boxes and cigarette packets in their live-drops. When an item is given without any acknowledgment it's called a brush pass. For example, walking past someone and slipping something into the other's coat pocket is a brush pass. When a spy leaves something for someone, such as an item inside a newspaper left on a park bench, this is called a dead drop.

Colonel Oleg Penkovsky helped the British gather a lot of information from the KGB.

house was bugged. Ruari brought the information to the British Embassy and sent it to Britain in diplomatic pouches. Those in the embassy developed the film, studied the documents and shared some of the information with the US CIA.

Although she and Penkovsky were no longer meeting in public, Janet continued to visit the park with her children and to stop in the secondhand shop. She wanted to make it appear as though these things were part of her regular routine in case the KGB was watching her as Penkovsky suspected. As it turned out, Penkovsky had good reason to be suspicious. Ruari and Janet

Chisholm had served in West Berlin at the same time as George Blake, whom they knew. Blake had reported Ruari as a spy to the KGB, and they had been watching the Chisholm family since the day they moved to Moscow.

After photographing Janet Chisholm walking into a strange apartment building just after one of their own colonels, the KGB had figured out Penkovsky was passing intelligence to the British. But the KGB didn't pounce on Penkovsky right away. Instead, they followed him and watched to see if he might lead them to other spies. When the KGB was satisfied that Penkovsky was only meeting with Janet, they made their move. Colonel Oleg Penkovsky was quietly arrested on 22 October 1962. Penkovsky was accused of treason and tried before the same judge who had found American U-2 pilot Gary Powers guilty. On 11 May 1963, Oleg Penkovsky was found guilty and sentenced to die. The court also pronounced Ruari and Janet Chisholm *personae non gratae*, or unwelcome people, and expelled them from the Soviet Union. As diplomats, they could not be tried for any crimes.

At the time of Oleg Penkovsky's arrest, US President John F Kennedy and Soviet leader Nikita Krushchev were embroiled in the Cuban Missile Crisis. For 13 days in October 1962, they were in a heated standoff over the Soviets' accumulation of nuclear-capable missiles in Cuba. Both sides feared the other would fire

The Cuban Missile Crisis was one of the most intense conflicts in world history.

the first weapon in a global nuclear war. But President Kennedy had an advantage over Krushchev. He had seen Oleg Penkovsky's pictures and reports and knew Krushchev didn't have the missile strength or range that he claimed. This information allowed Kennedy to hold out until Krushchev offered to remove the Cuban missiles if the Americans would agree not to invade Cuba.

A worldwide nuclear disaster was averted thanks in part to a Russian colonel with a chocolate box and a woman with a baby buggy.

DID YOU KNOW?

In 1962 the Soviets stockpiled nuclear
missiles that could reach the United
States from the Soviet's ally state, Cuba.
President John F Kennedy placed a naval
blockade around Cuba in October of 1962 to
prevent any further missile shipments from
arriving. Tensions between the two countries
increased, but a nuclear war was averted
when they reached an agreement whereby the
Soviet Union removed missiles from Cuba and
the United States agreed not to invade Cuba.

Pham Xuan An was beloved by those on both sides of the Vietnam conflict.

CHAPTER 5

PHAM XUAN AN: VIETNAM'S REPORTER SPY

Part of Pham Xuan An's name means "secret" in Vietnamese. This is fitting because he kept many secrets in his life, starting in the late 1940s in Vietnam. During that time period, Vietnam was part of a French colony known as French Indochina. Pham Xuan An organized student protests against the French occupiers and the Americans in Saigon. As an ardent nationalist, Pham Xuan An wanted an independent Vietnam free of outside control. He thought the Communist Party would bring this about, so he joined the movement. One day the Viet Minh, members of a group dedicated to Vietnamese independence and the advancement of communism, asked to meet with him. Pham Xuan An was told he had been selected for a more important role than student organizer. The Viet Minh planned to train him as an intelligence officer.

Pham Xuan An was an ideal spy candidate against the Americans because he had learned some English from

Many troops fought for a socialist Vietnam.

missionaries in his youth. From then on, whenever he met an
English speaker, he asked that person to help him study English.
People were happy to help the friendly, hard-working young man.
As a cover for his real work, the Viet Minh directed Pham Xuan An
to study journalism and learn more about American customs.

IT HELPS TO HAVE FRIENDS

In an odd twist of fate, the people who arranged Pham Xuan An's travel and college tuition in the United States were both involved in the CIA and working against the Viet Minh to stop the spread of communism. Pham Xuan An met one of these men, Colonel Edward Lansdale, while working as a Vietnamese translator for him. Lansdale took an immediate liking to An and offered to send him to intelligence school to train as a CIA spy.

As An was already involved in intelligence for the other side, he instead asked him for help in becoming a journalist. Through Lansdale's contacts at the Asia Foundation, arrangements were made for An to study in the United States. Another of Pham Xuan An's friends, Mills Brandes, who unbeknownst to An was a CIA operative, gave him names of family and friends in the United States to contact once he arrived there.

So, with the unwitting help of the CIA, the Viet Minh's secret spy, Pham Xuan An, arrived in sunny California on 12 October 1957, to study journalism at Orange Coast College in Costa Mesa. Pham Xuan An loved journalism and loved life in the United States even more. He wrote for the student newspaper, lived in the dorms, enjoyed dances and luaus, visited Disneyland and bought a second-hand car. He made many friends and was very popular. After a summer internship at the *Sacramento Bee* newspaper, Pham Xuan An drove across the country for a second internship at the

United Nations. After turning down a job teaching Vietnamese at the Department of Defence language school in Monterey, California, Pham Xuan An returned to his homeland to begin his cover identity as a journalist.

In Vietnam he got a job as an assistant with the news agency Reuters, serving as a translator and explaining Vietnamese politics and culture. He also worked for the *Vietnam Press* as a reporter and journalism teacher for other spies to help them establish cover identities as reporters. But Pham Xuan An took journalism almost as seriously as he did spying. He complained that the spies he taught didn't take their journalism classes seriously and would quickly be discovered.

VIETNAM WAR

The Vietnam War (also known as the Second Indochina War) was waged from 1 November 1955 to 30 April 1975. The country of Vietnam was divided into North Vietnam, known as the Democratic Republic of Vietnam, and South Vietnam. The North was supported by the Soviet Union, China and other communist countries. The South was backed by the United States, South Korea, Australia and other countries wanting to fend off the advancement of communism. Americans refer to the events of 30 April 1975, as "The Fall of Saigon," while some Vietnamese, especially in the North, refer to it as "Reunification Day."

Pham Xuan An was so good at journalism he later worked for *Time* magazine in Vietnam, covering the war as a full-time correspondent rather than a local assistant. He knew everyone in politics and the military. His predictions of North Vietnamese tactics were always spot on, much to the astonishment of other *Time* reporters. Some of his colleagues felt certain he worked for the CIA because his information was always so good. Of course, it helped that he knew exactly what the North Vietnamese planned because he was secretly one of their colonels.

Pham Xuan An often disappeared from his journalism job for days at a time. He explained his absences by also working as a dog trainer, saying he had to work at his other job. If anyone questioned him further he'd hint at visiting a secret lover. In reality, he did have to work at his other job, travelling to meet with the Vietcong, checking drop sites for messages and processing reports of American troop movements he gathered as a journalist.

SPRING ROLLS, SPY-STYLE

He relayed messages in more clandestine ways as well. After photographing sensitive documents for the Vietcong, he rolled the undeveloped film in spring roll wrappers, then tied the spring rolls together with brown paper on which he had written in invisible ink. He took his dogs out for a stroll in the local open-air market stalls and met his contact. The two chatted about the goods on

DID YOU KNOW?

Pham Xuan An made invisible ink himself.
He placed a few grains of rice and a bit
of water in a spoon. Then he heated the
spoon over a fire until the rice turned into
liquid. He then dipped a dry pen into it
and used the liquid rice to write invisible
messages. When his wrapping-paper messages
were received, another agent would brush an
iodine mixture over the paper to view the
secret message.

display. Pham Xuan An produced the spring rolls, pretending he had bought them at the open-air market, and offered them to his contact. She would then take them and hand them over to the military.

As the Vietnam War progressed, the North grew stronger and it became apparent the Vietcong would soon take over Saigon in South Vietnam. Journalists scrambled to get out of the country. *Time* magazine offered to fly Pham Xuan An and his family out of Vietnam. Although a man in An's position as a colonel had little to fear from the North's advance, he sent his wife and children to the United States aboard a CBS News aeroplane, fearing a door-to-door gun battle. Pham Xuan An himself stayed behind, claiming he needed to take care of his aging mother. He brought her to a room abandoned by one of his fleeing colleagues at the Continental Hotel to await the arrival of his fellow North Vietnamese.

It didn't take long for them to arrive. On 29 April 1975, Armed Forces radio in Saigon played Bing Crosby's song "White Christmas" over and over. It was the signal that all US personnel must evacuate immediately.

Although Pham Xuan An supported the Vietcong, he was extremely loyal to his American friends. When An realized one of them still hadn't left, he rushed him to the American Embassy and pushed him under the gate so his friend could evacuate from one of

When the North Vietnamese captured Saigon,
many Americans had to flee.

the last rooftop helicopters before Saigon was completely taken over

by the North Vietnamese.

The following day, 30 April 1975, An was the lone employee

of *Time* magazine in Vietnam. He sent a message stating, "All

American correspondents evacuated ... *Time* is now manned by

Pham Xuan An." Within 24 hours the North Vietnamese took over South Vietnam and hoisted their flag over Saigon.

Nearly two decades later, Pham Xuan An's son An Pham wanted to study journalism just like his father had done in the United States. By then Pham Xuan An's spying had long been revealed. Although his former colleagues knew of his deceit, they held him in high esteem as a journalist. So, they clubbed together to arrange for his son to study journalism at the University of North Carolina at Chapel Hill. Later, when Pham Xuan An died, many of the journalists he once worked with travelled to Vietnam to attend his funeral. They came to pay their last respects to a man they considered their colleague.

TIMELINE

26 May 1938
House Un-American Activities Committee is created

10 May 1940
Germany invades the Netherlands

August 1945
Korea is divided into North Korea and South Korea

2 September 1945
World War II ends

23 May 1949
Germany is officially divided into West Germany (Federal Republic of Germany) and East Germany (German Democratic Republic)

January 1950
Klaus Fuchs admits to giving atomic secrets to the Soviets

February 1950
Wisconsin Senator Joseph McCarthy claims in a speech to have a list of spies who are members of the Communist Party

25 June 1950
North Korea invades South Korea, beginning the Korean War

17 July 1950
Julius Rosenberg is arrested for spying

11 August 1950
Ethel Rosenberg is arrested for spying

6 March 1951
Julius and Ethel Rosenbergl, as well as Morton Sobell, go on trial

14 June 1953
Michael Rosenberg, son of Julius and Ethel, delivers a letter to President Eisenhower asking for clemency for his parents

17 June 1953
The Rosenbergs' executions are temporarily stayed

19 June 1953
The Rosenbergs' stay of execution is revoked. Julius Rosenberg dies in the electric chair, followed immediately by his wife.

27 July 1953
The Korean War ends. North Korea and South Korea remain divided.

1 November 1955
Vietnam is divided into North and South Vietnam. The Vietnam War begins.

January 1956
Gary Powers is hired by the CIA

June 1957
Colonel Rudolf Abel is arrested in the United States for being a Soviet spy

12 October 1957
Pham Xuan An arrives in California to study journalism

1 May 1960
Gary Powers is captured in the Soviet Union

May 1960
Soviet Premier Nikita Khrushchev promises Cuba he will defend it with Soviet missiles

2 July 1961
Janet Chisholm and Oleg Penkovsky meet in a Moscow park

13 August 1961
Construction begins on the Berlin Wall dividing the German city of Berlin into East Berlin and West Berlin

10 February 1962
Gary Powers and Frederic L Pryor are swapped for Colonel Rudolf Abel

22 October 1962
Oleg Penkovsky is arrested for passing secrets to the British

22-28 October 1962
The Cuban Missile Crisis

11 May 1963
Oleg Penkovsky is sentenced to die

March 1965
First US combat troops sent to Vietnam

30 April 1975
The Vietnam War ends with Saigon falling to the North Vietnamese

9 November 1989
The Berlin Wall falls

GLOSSARY

alias different name for someone

catastrophic terrible; causing major harm

clandestine secret

deceit lies or dishonesty

decipher uncover or find the meaning

deliberations conversations or thoughts to come to a decision

dignitary someone with a high rank or a high position

diplomatic pouch container sent to an embassy that isn't subject
to inspection

drops place where spies leave information for one another

Eastern bloc group of countries under Soviet rule until the collapse of
Soviet communism. Countries included the USSR, Poland, Albania, Ukraine,
East Germany, Czechoslovakia, Hungary, Romania, Bulgaria and Yugoslavia.

fascism government system of rule by a dictator, in which people are not
permitted to challenge the country's authority

glider aircraft that flies without an engine

hostile unfriendly

intelligence secret information gathered about an enemy

intercept stop something or someone before the destination is reached

intern confine or imprison, most often during a war

lenient not being strict; providing a lot of freedom

microfilm and microdots very small photos

Resistance movement that is counter to a system in power

treachery betraying a friend or country with harmful acts or words

tuition school fees

visa stamp on a passport that allows the owner to travel into a country
for a time

ADDITIONAL RESOURCES

FURTHER READING

Cold War Spies (Wartime Spies), Michael E Goodman (Creative Paperbacks, 2016)

Did Anything Good Come Out of the Cold War?, Paul Mason (Wayland, 2015)

Simple History: The Cold War, Daniel Turner (CreateSpace Independent Publishing Platform, 2016)

WEBSITES

www.ducksters.com/history/cold_war/summary.php
Learn about the events and leaders of the cold war through interesting articles and fun activities.

www.mi5.gov.uk/the-cold-war
Information on the part British Intelligence played in the Cold War.

www.nationalarchives.gov.uk/education/coldwar
Find out more about the Cold War in the United Kingdom including the location of a real nuclear bunker.

1. The judge in the Rosenberg trial referred to their "treason" in his decision. Look up the word "treason" in the dictionary. Were the Rosenbergs guilty of treason or not? Cite evidence from the text to back up your opinion.

2. Some of Pham Xuan An's former American journalist colleagues raised money to send his son to journalism school in the United States. Others felt Pham Xuan An betrayed their trust and exploited their friendship. Can you understand from the text why some of his colleagues remained loyal to Pham Xuan An even after learning he was a spy?

3. Summarize how Oleg Penkovsky and Janet Chisholm influenced the outcome of the Cuban Missile Crisis. If the two had never met, how might today's world be different? Find other sources to back up your argument.

SOURCE NOTES

p. 13, lines 8–10, Whittell, Giles. *Bridge of Spies: A True Story of the Cold War.* New York: Broadway Books, 2010, p. 201.

p. 16, lines 7–8, Powers, Francis Gary and Curt Gentry. *Operation Overflight: The U-2 Spy Pilot Tells His Story for the First Time.* ebook. New York: Holt, Rinehart and Winston, 1970, p. 237.

p. 26, lines 3–8, Meeropol, Robert and Michael Meeropol. *We Are Your Sons: The Legacy of Ethel and Julius Rosenberg.* Boston: Houghton Mifflin, 1975, p. 34.

p. 29, lines 4–5, Rosenberg, Julius and Ethel. *The Rosenberg Letters.* Ed. Michael Meeropol. ebook. New York: Garland Publishing, 1994, p. 704.

p. 33, line 20, Blake, George. *No Other Choice: An Autobiography.* New York: Simon & Schuster, 1990, p. 144.

p. 36, lines 1–3, Blake, George. *No Other Choice: An Autobiography.* New York: Simon & Schuster, 1990, p. 198.

p. 42, lines 20–21, Schecter, Jerrold L. and Peter Deriabin. *The Spy Who Saved the World: How a Soviet Colonel Changed the Course of the Cold War.* New York: C. Scribner's Sons, 1992, pp. 300–301.

p. 56–57, lines 4–5, 1, Berman, Larry. *Perfect Spy: The Incredible Double Life of Pham Xuan An, Time Magazine Reporter and Vietnamese Communist Agent.* New York: Smithsonian Books / Collins, 2007, p. 233.

SELECT BIBLIOGRAPHY

Bass, Thomas. "The Spy Who Loved Us—The New Yorker." *The New Yorker*. May 23, 2005. Accessed April 3, 2016. http://www.newyorker.com/magazine/2005/05/23/the-spy-who-loved-us

Berman, Larry. *Perfect Spy: The Incredible Double Life of Pham Xuan An, Time Magazine Reporter and Vietnamese Communist Agent*. New York: Smithsonian Books/Collins, 2007.

Blake, George. *No Other Choice: An Autobiography*. New York: Simon & Schuster, 1990.

Bourke, Seán. *The Springing of George Blake*. New York: Viking Press, 1970.

Meeropol, Robert and Michael Meeropol. *We Are Your Sons: The Legacy of Ethel and Julius Rosenberg*. Boston: Houghton Mifflin, 1975.

Powers, Francis Gary and Curt Gentry. *Operation Overflight: The U-2 Spy Pilot Tells His Story for the First Time*. New York: Holt, Rinehart and Winston, 1970.

Powers, Francis Gary and Curt Gentry. *Operation Overflight: The U-2 Spy Pilot Tells His Story for the First Time*. ebook. New York: Holt, Rinehart and Winston, 1970.

Rosenberg, Julius and Ethel. *The Rosenberg Letters*. Ed. Michael Meeropol. ebook. New York: Garland Publishing, 1994.

Schecter, Jerrold L. and Peter Deriabin. *The Spy Who Saved the World: How a Soviet Colonel Changed the Course of the Cold War*. New York: C. Scribner's Sons, 1992.

Whittell, Giles. *Bridge of Spies: A True Story of the Cold War*. New York: Broadway Books, 2010.

ABOUT THE AUTHOR

Rebecca Langston-George is the author of ten books including *Orphan Trains: Taking the Rails to a New Life*. When she's not writing she works as an elementary school teacher in California's Central Valley and volunteers as the assistant regional advisor for the Society of Children's Book Writers and Illustrators.